Anglican Foundations 11

I0172327

THE ANGLICAN ORDINAL

GOSPEL PRIORITIES FOR CHURCH OF ENGLAND MINISTRY

ANDREW ATHERSTONE

The Latimer Trust

Acknowledgments

Thanks especially to those who have engaged with this material in various forms, in seminar and chapel at Wycliffe Hall, Oxford; at Diocesan Evangelical Fellowships in Carlisle, Hereford, and Salisbury; and at the Latimer Trust Conference. Particular thanks to Wycliffe ordinands for their insightful criticisms on the full text – Laura Collingridge, Aron Donaldson, Thomas Fink-Jensen, Phil Keen, and Charmaine Muir – and for further suggestions from Gerald Bray, Martin Davie, Sarah Finch, Johnny Juckes, and Ed Moll.

Wycliffe Hall, Oxford
January 2020

Contents Page

INTRODUCTION

This brief Latimer Study is written with the conviction that there is no better handbook for Anglican ministry than the Anglican ordinal – the authorized liturgy for ordaining new ministers. As hundreds of new clergy are ordained in the Church of England every year, and as older churches are strengthened and revitalized and newer churches are pioneered in many different communities, where do we look for sustainable ministry models and clear theological priorities? There is no shortage of paperbacks about Anglican ministry, and about Christian leadership more broadly, flowing from the printing presses at a rapid rate.[1] But no text has shaped Anglican ministry more than the ordinal. It is a beautifully clear and succinct ministry handbook, full of wisdom drawn by the Anglican Reformers from the pages of the Bible. This booklet offers a simple exposition of its primary themes.

This study has three groups of readers in mind. First, it is intended as a guide for ordinands or those exploring their vocation, who must wrestle prayerfully with the ordination liturgy during the discernment process and their preparation for the great day of ordination itself. Second, it is intended to assist bishops, Diocesan Directors of Ordinands, members of

---

[1] See, for example, Christopher Cocksworth and Rosalind Brown, *Being a Priest Today: Exploring Priestly Identity* (second edition, Norwich: Canterbury Press, 2006); John Pritchard, *The Life and Work of a Priest* (London: SPCK, 2007); Steven Croft, *Ministry in Three Dimensions: Ordination and Leadership in the Local Church* (new edition, London: Darton, Longman and Todd, 2008); Alan Billings, *Making God Possible: The Task of Ordained Ministry Present and Future* (London: SPCK, 2010); Robin Ward, *On Christian Priesthood* (London: Continuum, 2011); Graham Tomlin, *The Widening Circle: Priesthood as God's Way of Blessing the World* (London: SPCK, 2014); Magdalen Smith, *Steel Angels: The Personal Qualities of a Priest* (London: SPCK, 2014); Emma Percy, *What Clergy Do: Especially When It Looks Like Nothing* (London: SPCK, 2014); Jessica Martin and Sarah Coakley (eds), *For God's Sake: Re-Imagining Priesthood and Prayer in a Changing Church* (Norwich: Canterbury Press, 2016); Jamie Harrison and Robert Innes (eds), *Clergy in a Complex Age: Responses to the Guidelines for the Professional Conduct of the Clergy* (London: SPCK, 2016); David Hoyle, *The Pattern of our Calling: Ministry Yesterday, Today and Tomorrow* (London: SCM Press, 2016); Martyn Percy et al (eds), *The Study of Ministry: A Comprehensive Survey of Theory and Best Practice* (London: SPCK, 2019).

Bishops Advisory Panels, and theological educators, who are responsible for identifying and training those called to ordination in the Church of England. Third, this booklet is written as an *aide memoire* for clergy, to encourage prayerful reflection upon the promises made at the launch of their public ministries, as an ordination MOT or 'ministry medical';[2] as well as for congregations wanting to know what they should look for in a vicar.

What sort of ministers does the Church of England need today? The Anglican ordinal provides the answers. Canon A5 declares:

> The doctrine of the Church of England is grounded in the Holy Scriptures, and in such teachings of the ancient Fathers and Councils of the Church as are agreeable to the said Scriptures. In particular, such doctrine is to be found in the Thirty-Nine Articles of Religion, the *Book of Common Prayer*, and the Ordinal.

The Thirty-Nine Articles and Prayer Book are well known, but the ordinal less so. Yet Canon A5 instructs us that it is the place to look if we want to understand the Anglican doctrine of ministry. The official standard is the ordinal attached to the 1662 *Book of Common Prayer* (derived largely from Archbishop Thomas Cranmer's ordinal of 1552), though a new *Common Worship* ordinal has been in widespread use since 2005 as a popular alternative.[3] Both texts are examined here, side by side.

---

[2] Jonathan Griffiths, *The Ministry Medical: A Health-Check from 2 Timothy* (Fearn, Ross-shire: Christian Focus, 2013).

[3] For commentary on ordinal revision, see especially, Paul F. Bradshaw, *The Anglican Ordinal: Its History and Development from the Reformation to the Present Day* (London: SPCK, 1971); Colin Buchanan, *Ordination Rites in Common Worship* (Cambridge: Grove Books, 2006); Ronald L. Dowling and David R. Holeton (eds), *Equipping the Saints: Ordination in Anglicanism Today* (Dublin: Columba Press, 2006); Paul F. Bradshaw, *Rites of Ordination: Their History and Theology* (London: SPCK, 2014). For the *Book of Common Prayer* and *Common Worship* ordinals side by side, see *Common Worship: Ordination Services, Study Edition* (London: Church House Publishing, 2007); for comparisons across the Anglican Communion, see Phillip Tovey, *Anglican Ordination Rites* (Kindle Direct Publishing, 2019).

The ordination service falls broadly into three parts:

- **Exhortation** – a declaration about the nature of ordained ministry, with a personal exhortation of the candidates. In *Common Worship* deacons, priests (also called presbyters), and bishops are all exhorted, though in the *Book of Common Prayer* only priests are.

- **Examination** – the candidates are interrogated about their ministry priorities, with a series of searching questions, and they make solemn promises.

- **Ordination** – the candidates are admitted to their new order of ministry, with invocation of the Holy Spirit, the laying-on-of-hands, and the gift of a Bible.

These three parts will be expounded in turn, with brief commentary.

1. Exhortation

At the heart of the ordination service, after opening prayers and Bible readings, the bishop exhorts the ordinands concerning the ministry they are about to enter. This chapter examines the exhortation to presbyters.[1] It is a particularly serious and heart-warming address, a portrait of Anglican ministry resonant with biblical imagery, and each sentence is worth weighing carefully. The liturgical texts are laid out here in full for easy comparison.

The Texts

The *Book of Common Prayer* exhortation to presbyters reads as follows:

> Ye have heard, brethren, as well in your private examination, as in the exhortation which was now made to you, and in the holy lessons taken out of the Gospel, and the writings of the apostles, of what dignity, and of how great importance this office is, whereunto ye are called. And now again we exhort you, in the name of our Lord Jesus Christ, that ye have in remembrance, into how high a dignity, and to how weighty an office and charge ye are called: that is to say, to be messengers, watchmen, and stewards of the Lord; to teach, and to premonish, to feed and provide for the Lord's family; to seek for Christ's sheep that are dispersed abroad, and for his children who are in the midst of this naughty world, that they may be saved through Christ for ever.
>
> Have always therefore printed in your remembrance, how great a treasure is committed to your charge. For they are the sheep of Christ, which he bought with his death, and for whom he shed his blood. The Church and congregation whom you must serve, is his spouse, and his body. And if it shall happen that the same Church, or any member thereof, do take any hurt or hindrance by reason of your negligence, ye know the greatness of the fault, and also the horrible punishment that will ensue. Wherefore consider with

---

[1] For the sake of theological clarity, this booklet adopts the terminology of 'presbyters' rather than 'priests', used interchangeably in the *Common Worship* ordinal. For an explanation of the ambiguities, see Chapter 3.

yourselves the end of the ministry towards the children of God, towards the spouse and body of Christ; and see that ye never cease your labour, your care and diligence, until ye have done all that lieth in you, according to your bounden duty, to bring all such as are or shall be committed to your charge, unto that agreement in the faith and knowledge of God, and to that ripeness and perfectness of age in Christ, that there be no place left among you, either for error in religion, or for viciousness in life.

Forasmuch then as your office is both of so great excellency, and of so great difficulty, ye see with how great care and study ye ought to apply yourselves, as well to show yourselves dutiful and thankful unto that Lord, who hath placed you in so high a dignity; as also to beware that neither you yourselves offend, nor be occasion that others offend. Howbeit, ye cannot have a mind and will thereto of yourselves; for that will and ability is given of God alone: therefore ye ought, and have need, to pray earnestly for his Holy Spirit. And seeing that ye cannot by any other means compass the doing of so weighty a work, pertaining to the salvation of man, but with doctrine and exhortation taken out of the Holy Scriptures, and with a life agreeable to the same; consider how studious ye ought to be in reading and learning the Scriptures, and in framing the manners both of yourselves, and of them that specially pertain unto you, according to the rule of the same Scriptures; and for this self-same cause, how ye ought to forsake and set aside, as much as ye may, all worldly cares and studies.

We have good hope that ye have well weighed these things with yourselves, long before this time; and that ye have clearly determined, by God's grace, to give yourselves wholly to this office, whereunto it hath pleased God to call you: so that, as much as lieth in you, ye will apply yourselves wholly to this one thing, and draw all your cares and studies this way; and that ye will continually pray to God the Father, by the mediation of our only Saviour Jesus Christ, for the heavenly assistance of the Holy Ghost; that, by daily reading and weighing the Scriptures, ye may wax riper and stronger in your ministry; and that ye may so endeavour yourselves, from time to time, to sanctify the lives of you and yours, and to fashion them after the rule and doctrine of Christ, that ye may be wholesome and godly examples and patterns for the people to follow.

In *Common Worship*, the exhortation to presbyters follows a similar line, with some direct word-for-word parallels. However, unlike the *Book of Common Prayer*, it recognizes the ministry of the whole people of God – laity and clergy together – and frames ordination within that wider context. Its opens with a beautiful description of the whole Church taken from 1 Peter 2:9, addressed not just to the ordinands but to the whole congregation:

> God calls his people to follow Christ, and forms us into a royal priesthood, a holy nation, to declare the wonderful deeds of him who has called us out of darkness into his marvellous light. The Church is the body of Christ, the people of God and the dwelling-place of the Holy Spirit. In baptism the whole Church is summoned to witness to God's love and to work for the coming of his kingdom.
>
> To serve this royal priesthood, God has given particular ministries. Priests are ordained to lead God's people in the offering of praise and the proclamation of the gospel. They share with the bishop in the oversight of the Church, delighting in its beauty and rejoicing in its well-being. They are to set the example of the Good Shepherd always before them as the pattern of their calling. With the bishop and their fellow presbyters, they are to sustain the community of the faithful by the ministry of word and sacrament, that we all may grow into the fullness of Christ and be a living sacrifice acceptable to God. . . .
>
> . . . Priests are called to be servants and shepherds among the people to whom they are sent. With their bishop and fellow ministers, they are to proclaim the word of the Lord and to watch for the signs of God's new creation. They are to be messengers, watchmen and stewards of the Lord; they are to teach and to admonish, to feed and provide for his family, to search for his children in the wilderness of this world's temptations, and to guide them through its confusions, that they may be saved through Christ for ever. Formed by the

word, they are to call their hearers to repentance and to declare in Christ's name the absolution and forgiveness of their sins.

With all God's people, they are to tell the story of God's love. They are to baptize new disciples in the name of the Father, and of the Son, and of the Holy Spirit, and to walk with them in the way of Christ, nurturing them in the faith. They are to unfold the Scriptures, to preach the word in season and out of season, and to declare the mighty acts of God. They are to preside at the Lord's table and lead his people in worship, offering with them a spiritual sacrifice of praise and thanksgiving. They are to bless the people in God's name. They are to resist evil, support the weak, defend the poor, and intercede for all in need. They are to minister to the sick and prepare the dying for their death. Guided by the Spirit, they are to discern and foster the gifts of all God's people, that the whole Church may be built up in unity and faith.

In *Common Worship* the bishop then turns to address the ordinands directly:

We trust that long ago you began to weigh and ponder all this, and that you are fully determined, by the grace of God, to devote yourself wholly to his service, so that as you daily follow the rule and teaching of our Lord and grow into his likeness, God may sanctify the lives of all with whom you have to do. . . .

. . . In the name of our Lord we bid you remember the greatness of the trust that is now to be committed to your charge. Remember always with thanksgiving that the treasure now to be entrusted to you is Christ's own flock, bought by the shedding of his blood on the cross. It is to him that you will render account for your stewardship of his people.

You cannot bear the weight of this calling in your own strength, but only by the grace and power of God. Pray therefore that your heart may daily be enlarged and your understanding of the Scriptures enlightened. Pray earnestly for the gift of the Holy Spirit.

Compared to the *Book of Common Prayer*, the *Common Worship* description of presbyteral ministry is more diffuse, and now includes liturgical functions (absolving, blessing, presiding at the Lord's table, leading public worship). Nevertheless, both exhortations have in common four great biblical metaphors of the work of the presbyter in the local church. Three appear together in the famous phrase, 'messengers, watchmen, and stewards of the Lord'. The fourth is of the presbyter as shepherd. We will consider each briefly in turn.[2]

Messengers

The first biblical image is of the presbyter as a messenger. The Old Testament frequently describes the prophet or priest in this way. 'Then Haggai, the messenger of the Lord, spoke to the people with the Lord's message' (Haggai 1:13); 'The lips of a priest should guard knowledge, and people should seek instruction from his mouth, for he is the messenger of the Lord of hosts' (Malachi 2:7). Isaiah conveys the great joy of those who see the messenger coming: 'How beautiful upon the mountains are the feet of him who brings good news, who publishes peace, who brings good news of happiness, who publishes salvation, who says to Zion, "Your God reigns"' (Isaiah 52:7). The meaning of the metaphor is obvious: someone entrusted with a message from the Lord, to deliver to the people. In the New Testament it is picked up by a range of images. For example, Paul describes himself as a 'herald' of the gospel (1 Timothy 2:7), akin to a town crier in the marketplace, and as an 'ambassador' for Christ, with a message of reconciliation, 'God making his appeal through us' (2 Corinthians 5:20). In expounding the phrase 'ministers of Christ' (1 Corinthians 4:1) in his *Horae Homileticae*, Charles Simeon (1759-1836), vicar of Holy Trinity, Cambridge, notes:

> They are sent by Christ. They come not of themselves, but as commissioned by him. It is his message that they bring; his will that they perform. By them it is that he speaks to men.

---

[2] The commentary in this chapter owes a great deal to Martin Parsons, *The Ordinal: An Exposition of the Ordination Services* (London: Hodder and Stoughton, 1964).

As earthly kings are represented by their ambassador, and speak by them in foreign courts, so the Lord Jesus Christ himself speaks by his ministers: they stand in his stead: they speak in his name: their word is not their own, but his; and must be received, 'not as the word of men, but, as it is in truth, the word of God'.[3]

This image of presbyters as messengers has pride of place in the Anglican ordinal. It has at least three straightforward implications: (1) presbyters must know and understand the gospel message; (2) presbyters must obediently deliver the message of the gospel, with clarity, wherever they are sent; (3) presbyters are to be judged not on the response of their hearers, but on their own faithfulness in delivering the message truthfully.

In an address entitled 'Thoughts on the Ministry' (1884), the first Bishop of Liverpool, J. C. Ryle (1816-1900), exhorted the clergy: 'We have got to deliver our Master's message – to keep back nothing that is profitable – to declare all the counsel of God. If we tell our congregations *less* than the truth or *more* than the truth, we may ruin for ever immortal souls. Life and death are in the power of the preacher's tongue.'[4] A lover of military metaphors, Ryle likened the ordained minister to 'a trumpeter in the army of Christ', who must ensure their bugle sounds a clear note so the troops will understand the message (1 Corinthians 4:8):

In military matters, common sense points out that the trumpeter of a regiment is perfectly useless if he does not know how to use the instrument which is placed in his hands. He may be duly entered on the muster roll, and occupy a conspicuous position, and wear a splendid uniform; but if he does not know how to carry out the orders of his commanding officer, if he can neither give the sound to advance or retreat, to charge, to halt, or to retire, he is more

---

[3] Charles Simeon, *Horae Homileticae: or Discourses (Principally in the Form of Skeletons) Now First Digested into One Continued Series, and Forming a Commentary Upon Every Book of the Old and New Testament* (21 vols, London: Holdsworth and Ball, 1833), vol. 16, skeleton 1951, p. 143.
[4] 'Thoughts on the Ministry', in J. C. Ryle, *Principles for Churchmen: A Manual of Positive Statements on Doubtful or Disputed Points* (London: William Hunt, 1884), p. 155.

likely to do harm than good. In fact, he is likely, in the day of battle, to throw the whole force into confusion.

'Now, in the great campaign of the Church of Christ', Ryle explained, 'it is just the same with the ministers of the everlasting gospel.' If their message is 'uncertain, confused, and indistinct', not helping anyone towards heaven, then 'in spite of orders, licence, and commission, such a minister is as useless as the ignorant regimental trumpeter.[5] The bishop prayed: 'Lord, send forth more labourers into Thy harvest! Raise up many more faithful ministers in Thy Church! Revive Thy work in England! Give us more trumpeters of the Gospel!'[6] In an earlier address from the 1850s on *The Cross*, Ryle multiplied metaphors to describe the church which neglects to proclaim the message of Christ crucified with clarity and vigour. Such a church, and such a ministry, is

> little better than a cumberer of the ground, a dead carcase, a well without water, a barren fig tree, a sleeping watchman, a silent trumpet, a dumb witness, an ambassador without terms of peace, a messenger without tidings, a lighthouse without fire, a stumbling-block to weak believers, a comfort to infidels, a hot-bed for formalism, a joy to the devil, and an offence to God.[7]

Griffith Thomas (1861-1924) put it succinctly, in his addresses to ordinands at Wycliffe Hall, Oxford, in the early twentieth century. 'Herein lies the supreme secret of Christian ministry', he explained – the person who 'knows God, who knows God's truth, who knows by experience what Christianity is, and who intends at all costs to tell what he knows and give what he has received.' The minister who is confused or doubtful 'can never be a messenger of the Lord of Hosts'.[8] Presbyters are to be confident in their gospel proclamation: not adding to or subtracting from the message, not muffling or confusing it, but delivering it just as the Lord has told them.

---

[5] 'Thoughts on the Ministry', p. 165.
[6] 'Thoughts on the Ministry', p. 172.
[7] J. C. Ryle, *The Cross: A Tract for the Times* (Ipswich: Hunt, 1852), p. 26.
[8] W. H. Griffith Thomas, *The Work of the Ministry* (London: Hodder and Stoughton, 1911), p. 165.

Watchmen / Sentinels

The second biblical image adopted by the Anglican ordinal is of presbyters as 'watchmen'. This word is retained in the gender-inclusive *Common Worship* ordinal because of its evocative Old Testament resonance.[9] 'Sentinels' is a good alternative.

In ancient Israel, the watchman was often stationed out in the fields, in a tower, watching over the farm or the vineyard, on guard against wild animals, fires, or thieves. In the city, they watched from the ramparts or the citadel, looking out for danger (like the arrival of marauding armies) or to identify a runner bringing news. We get a glimpse of this vital task in 2 Samuel 18:24-27. In the Old Testament, it became a familiar metaphor for prophetic ministry. Habakkuk declared: 'I will take my stand at my watchpost and station myself on the tower, and look out to see what the Lord will say to me' (Habakkuk 2:1). The image is of someone climbing up to a high vantage point, to get the best view of the horizon, and waiting to hear the Lord's voice. Ezekiel was explicitly commissioned by the Lord as 'a watchman for the house of Israel', charged with declaring God's word. The prophet's role was to watch for the judgment of the Lord and (metaphorically) to blow the trumpet at the first sign of danger, to warn the people to flee from the wrath of God and to seek salvation (Ezekiel 3:16-21, 33:1-9). What a solemn, weighty ministry! Sentinels must be alert, faithful to their calling, not negligent in their ministry, because the consequences are huge – indeed eternal destinies are at stake. The ordained minister is in that sense a guardian of the people. The exhortation to presbyters in the *Book of Common Prayer* ordinal uses the old English word, 'to premonish' – that is, to warn people in advance about what is going to happen, before it is too late.

This image of Christian ministers as sentinels is picked up also in the New Testament. The Letter to the Hebrews urges: 'Obey your leaders and submit to them, for they are keeping watch over your souls, as those who will have to give an account' (Hebrews 13:17). A ministry of warning and admonishment was central to the way Paul understood his calling: 'Him [Christ] we proclaim, warning everyone and teaching everyone with all wisdom, that we may present everyone mature in Christ' (Colossians

---

[9] *Ordination Services: Report of the Revision Committee*, January 2005, GS 1535Y, paragraph 76.

1:28). He reminded the Ephesians elders: 'for three years I did not cease night or day to admonish everyone with tears' (Acts 20:31). As Martin Parsons (1907-1997) explains: 'to be a watchman requires a high degree, not only of pastoral oversight, but of prophetic insight'; the presbyter's role is 'to discern the signs of the times, to see more clearly than others God's purpose for the world', and thus be able to give the message with urgency.[10]

Here there is significant overlap between the duties of messengers and sentinels. They are not to be judged by the actions of their hearers, but on their diligence in delivering the message or sounding the alarm. The Bible does not measure ministry success by fruitfulness, but by faithfulness. Preaching in 1550 on the parable of the wedding feast (Matthew 22:1-14), Bishop Hugh Latimer (c.1485-1555) asked rhetorically why the king did not blame his servants for their limited success in recruiting suitable wedding guests. Latimer's answer was that the servants, like gospel preachers, had fulfilled their duty by issuing the invitations: 'They can do no more but call; God is he that must bring in'.[11] The bishop noticed that many clergy had ceased to prioritise preaching, and when asked why, they often gave the excuse that there was not enough fruit. Latimer retorted:

> A naughty answer: a very naughty answer. Thou art troubled with what God gave thee no charge of; and leavest undone that thou art charged with. God commandeth thee to preach ... if thou speak not, if thou warn not the wicked, that they turn and amend, they shall perish in their iniquities ... This text nippeth; this pincheth; this touchest the quick: 'He shall die in his wickedness, but I will require his blood at thy hand' [Ezekiel 3 and 33]. Hearken well to this, mark it well, ye curates; 'I will ask his blood at thy hand.' If you do not your office, if ye teach not the people, and warn them not, you shall be damned for it. If you do your office, you are discharged ...[12]

---

[10] Parsons, *The Ordinal*, pp. 50-1.
[11] 'Sermon Preached at Stamford' (1550), in *The Works of Hugh Latimer*, edited for the Parker Society by George Elwes Corrie (Cambridge: Cambridge University Press, 1844), p. 285.
[12] 'Sermon Preached at Stamford', p. 286.

It is the role of the Holy Spirit to open hearts and minds to the gospel (Luke 24:45, Acts 16:14); it is the duty of presbyters to open their mouths and speak what they have been told.

On one of Charles Simeon's visits to Edinburgh, he preached a memorable sermon on ministerial faithfulness, taking as an illustration the famous Inchkeith Lighthouse (built in 1803) on an island in the middle of the Firth of Forth. He imagined that the light went out, 'and that in consequence the coast was strewed with wrecks, and with dead and mangled bodies; and that the wailing of widows and orphans were everywhere heard.' The delinquent lighthouse-keeper was brought out to be interrogated by the court, to discover the cause of the disaster, until he confessed that he had been asleep. 'Asleep!', declared Simeon. One Scottish congregation member recalled: 'The way in which he made this "asleep!" burst on the ears of his audience, who were hanging in perfect stillness on his lips . . . I remember to this day.'[13] Simeon's point chimes with the priorities of the Anglican ordinal. Faithful Christian ministry, like the role of sentinels, is of supreme urgency because danger is at hand and lives are at stake.

Stewards

The third biblical image is of the presbyter as a steward – the overseer or manager of a grand house or an estate (for example, the parable in Luke 16:1-9). The steward has authority over others, perhaps over property and riches, but it is a delegated authority from their master. They have genuine responsibility to take initiatives, but their sole aim is to protect and multiply their master's possessions, for which they will have to give an account. To update the image for the twenty-first century, a steward is like a trustee – given something 'in trust' to look after on behalf of others.

The New Testament adopts this metaphor for Christian ministry. For example, to the church in Corinth, Paul defends his own ministry: 'This is how one should regard us, as servants of Christ and stewards of the mysteries of God. Moreover, it is required of stewards that they be found trustworthy' (1 Corinthians 4:1-2). In other words, he has been entrusted with the gospel message, and must guard it and pass it on faithfully. But

---

[13] Matthew Morris Preston, *Memoranda of the Rev. Charles Simeon* (London: Richard Watts, 1840), p. 49.

it is not only apostles who are stewards. So are those given oversight of local churches. Paul tells Titus that the presbyter-bishop is 'God's steward' (Titus 1:7). Therefore the Anglican ordinal readily adopts this image. The presbyter guards the congregation, taking care of God's church. The *Common Worship* ordinal puts it starkly: 'In the name of our Lord we bid you remember the greatness of the trust now to be committed to your charge. . . . It is to Christ that you will render account for your stewardship of his people.' The presbyter also guards the gospel, making sure it is handed on uncorrupted.

John Stott (1921-2011), rector of All Souls', Langham Place, in his classic study *The Preacher's Portrait* (1961), expounded the metaphor of preacher as steward. He observed:

> The steward is the trustee and dispenser of another person's goods. So the preacher is a steward of God's mysteries, that is, of the self-revelation which God has entrusted to men and which is now preserved in the Scriptures. The Christian preacher's message, therefore, is derived not directly from the mouth of God, as if he were a prophet or apostle, nor from his own mind, like the false prophets, nor undigested from the minds and mouths of others, like the babbler, but from the once revealed and now recorded Word of God, of which he is a privileged steward.[14]

Stott helpfully draws out four implications. First, there is motivation here for weary ministers, as under the Lord's commission. The gospel has been 'entrusted' to them by God, 'so we speak, not to please people, but to please God who tests our hearts' (1 Thessalonians 2:4). Paul felt under urgent obligation, having been 'entrusted with a stewardship': 'For necessity is laid upon me. Woe to me if I do not preach the gospel!' (1 Corinthians 9:16-17). Second, ministers are to 'guard the good deposit' entrusted to them, not adulterating it or subtracting from it (1 Timothy 6:20, 2 Timothy 1:14). The steward 'is not expected to feed the household out of his own pocket . . . by his own ingenuity', but faithfully to distribute

---

[14] 'A Steward: The Preacher's Message and Authority', in John Stott, *The Preacher's Portrait: Some New Testament Word Studies* (Grand Rapids, MI: Eerdmans, 1961), p. 17 (cited in Parsons, *The Ordinal*, p. 53).

the provisions which the Divine Householder has bountifully supplied.[15] Third the minister, like the steward, speaks with delegated authority. Fourth, ministers must immerse themselves in the Scriptures, just as the steward must 'make himself familiar with all the contents of his larder'.[16] Stott concludes that faithfulness is key: the steward must be faithful in studying and preaching the Word, faithful to the householder, faithful to the household, and faithful to the deposit committed to the steward's trust. 'May God make us faithful stewards!'[17]

Shepherds

The fourth biblical image picked up by the Anglican ordinal is of the presbyter as a shepherd, or pastor. Cranmer's ordinal in 1552 spoke of 'the messengers, the watchmen, the pastors, and the stewards of the Lord'. The word 'pastor' was omitted in 1662 because it had acquired anti-episcopal connotations during the Commonwealth period,[18] though the pastoral, shepherding metaphor is retained and driven home repeatedly.

All three Bible readings laid down in the *Book of Common Prayer* for presbyteral ordination emphasise this model of ministry:

- Ephesians 4:7-13, about the gift to the church of apostles, prophets, evangelists, and 'pastors and teachers', 'for the perfecting of the saints for the work of the ministry, for the edifying of the body of Christ . . .'

- Matthew 9:36-38: 'When Jesus saw the multitudes, he was moved with compassion on them, because they fainted, and were scattered abroad, as sheep having no shepherd. Then saith he unto his disciples, The harvest truly is plenteous, but the labourers are

---

[15] Stott, *The Preacher's Portrait*, pp. 23, 25.

[16] Stott, *The Preacher's Portrait*, p. 30.

[17] Stott, *The Preacher's Portrait*, p. 32.

[18] For the same reason, the petition in the 1552 Litany for God 'to illuminate all Bishops, Pastors, and Ministers of the Church with true knowledge and understanding of thy word', was altered in 1662 to 'all Bishops, Priests, and Deacons'. For Cranmer's original text, see *The First and Second Prayer Books of Edward VI* (London: Prayer Book Society, 1999).

few; pray ye therefore the Lord of the harvest, that he will send forth labourers into his harvest.'

- John 10:1-16, contrasting Jesus as the good shepherd who 'giveth his life for the sheep', with the 'hireling' who 'careth not for the sheep' and leaves them to be scattered and devoured by the wolf.

Within this rich picture of the presbyter as shepherd / pastor, there is an emphasis upon feeding the flock by teaching them the Word of God; deep compassion and care for the needy and oppressed; sacrificial service; protection of the sheep from dangerous adversaries or imposters; and a gathering in of those outside the fold. Pastoral and evangelistic ministry cannot be separated, and the Anglican ordinal refuses to draw a division between the two. As the bishop exhorts the presbyters, they are 'to seek for Christ's sheep that are dispersed abroad'. Jesus links the two ministries explicitly in Matthew 9 by connecting the shepherd with the labourer in the harvest field. Preaching on that text, John Jewel (1522-1571), Bishop of Salisbury, lamented:

> But the labourers are few. I say not, there be but few cardinals, few bishops, few priests that should be preachers, few archdeacons, few chancellors, few deans, few prebendaries, few vicars, few parish priests, few monks, few friars; for the number of these is almost infinite . . . The number of these is great; but, alas! the number of the labourers is very small. . . . The labourers are but few; but the destroyers and wasters are exceeding many; yea, such as should be the harvest-men most of all destroy the corn.[19]

It is excellent for the Church of England to aspire to increase the number of ordained ministers, but only if they are trained and deployed for the right work. To echo Bishop Jewel, it would be a tragedy if, after an effective recruitment drive, the ordinands were multitudinous but the labourers in the harvest remained few.

---

[19] 'Certain Sermons of Bishop Jewel', in *The Works of John Jewel*, edited for the Parker Society by John Ayre (4 vols, Cambridge: Cambridge University Press, 1845-50), vol.2, pp. 1019-20.

The true labourer, or the true shepherd, is a pioneer in evangelism. This is one of the presbyter's central responsibilities. Jesus' story of the lost sheep (Luke 15:3-7) offers a helpful parallel – although in many of our parishes the numbers are now reversed, with only one in the fold and 99 who are lost. The shepherd / pastor is to lead the search party, not ministering only to those within the church, but going out to reach the lost. The revised exhortation in the *Common Worship* ordinal continues this biblical emphasis:

> [Presbyters] are to set the example of the Good Shepherd always before them as the pattern of their calling. . . . They are to teach and to admonish, to feed and provide for the Lord's family, to search for his children in the wilderness of this world's temptations, and to guide them through its confusions, that they may be saved through Christ for ever. . . . Remember always with thanksgiving that the treasure now to be entrusted to you is Christ's own flock, bought by the shedding of his blood on the cross.

Here we see in Anglican ecclesiology considerable overlap between presbyteral and episcopal ministry. The 1662 ordinal prays that God would give grace to all bishops as 'the Pastors of thy Church'. The Bible readings laid down for their consecration include Acts 20:17-35 ('Take heed therefore unto yourselves, and to all the flock over which the Holy Ghost hath made you overseers') and John 21:15-17 (Jesus' command to Peter to 'Feed my sheep'). The new bishops are exhorted:

> Be to the flock of Christ a shepherd, not a wolf. Feed them, devour them not. Hold up the weak, heal the sick, bind up the broken, bring again the outcasts, seek the lost. Be so merciful, that you be not too remiss; so minister discipline, that you forget not mercy: that when the Chief Shepherd shall appear you may receive the never-fading crown of glory . . .

Here are deliberate echoes, even at the very point of episcopal consecration, of Peter's exhortation to presbyters (1 Peter 5:1-4). The ministry of shepherd / pastor with oversight of God's flock is shared between presbyters and bishops – indeed the New Testament often uses those terms interchangeably.

There is overlap also between the various biblical metaphors picked up by the Anglican ordinal. Isaiah combines the images of the sleeping watchman with the greedy and drunken shepherd, a terrible concoction. The prophet sarcastically invites the wild animals to come and devour the flock of God, because their guardians have neglected their duty (Isaiah 56:9-12). The Anglican Reformers mourned over the parlous state of pastoral ministry in the Church of England, and the ordinal was designed to raise the standard in line with biblical imperatives. 'It pitieth me', wrote Archbishop Cranmer in 1550, 'to see the simple and hungry flock of Christ led into corrupt pastures, to be carried blindfold they know not whither, and to be fed with poison in the stead of wholesome meats.' The antidote, he proclaimed, was for God's ministers 'to set forth his word truly unto his people' to the uttermost of their power, 'without respect of person, or regard of anything in the world, but of him alone'.[20] In December 1552, Bishop Latimer preached a Christmas sermon from Luke 2 in which he drew practical application from the shepherds who witnessed Jesus' birth, for Christian ministry:

> I would wish that clergymen – the curates, parsons, and vicars, the bishops, and all other spiritual persons – would learn this lesson by these poor shepherds; which is this, to abide by their flocks and by their sheep, to tarry amongst them, to be careful over them; not to run hither and thither after their own pleasure, but to tarry by their benefices and feed their sheep with the food of God's word, and to keep hospitality, and so to feed them both soul and body.

Latimer warned that the clergy had responsibility to feed 'God's lambs, which he bought with the death of his Son', but were woefully negligent in their duty of care.[21] A century later, the shocking pastoral neglect of the Anglican clergy was likewise exposed by John Milton's *Lycidas* (1637) with

---

[20] Preface (1550) to 'An Answer unto a Crafty and Sophistical Cavillation, Devised by Stephen Gardiner . . . Against the True and Godly Doctrine of the Most Holy Sacrament of the Body and Blood of our Saviour Jesus Christ', in *Writings and Disputations of Thomas Cranmer, Relative to the Sacrament of the Lord's Supper*, edited for the Parker Society by John Edmund Cox (Cambridge: Cambridge University Press, 1844), p. 6.
[21] 'Sermon Preached at Grimsthorpe' (1552), in *Sermons and Remains of Hugh Latimer*, edited for the Parker Society by George Elwes Corrie (Cambridge: Cambridge University Press, 1845), p. 120.

its famous lament, 'The hungry sheep look up, and are not fed.' Milton did not pull his punches in his indictment of those ordained as shepherds: they were no better than ignorant and greedy hirelings, who allowed the flock either to be torn to pieces by the wolf or to die of spiritual hunger and disease.[22]

The Anglican ordinal sets a high standard, in line with the New Testament, to which clergy are to be held accountable throughout their ministries. Before Thomas Wilson (1663-1755), long-serving Bishop of Sodor and Man, instituted clergy into new parochial responsibilities in his diocese, he prayed earnestly for them. The petition survives among his *Sacra Privata*, and begins as follow:

> O great and good Shepherd, may this person whom I am going to send into Thy service love Thee so sincerely, that for Thy sake he may have a tender concern for Thy flock: that he may diligently feed and watch over them, that the enemy may not rob Thee of any of those sheep which Thou hast purchased with Thy blood. They are Thine, O save them for Thy mercy's sake, and let none of them be lost or go astray through any fault of mine, or of those whom I send into Thy service.[23]

Here Wilson acknowledges his double responsibility as bishop for protecting the church, both by his own teaching, and by licensing only those clergy who were able and willing to shepherd the flock.

High Calling and Weighty Work

The ordinal's exhortation to presbyters reiterates, again and again, that this ministry is an awesome responsibility of 'great importance'. 'And now again we exhort you, in the name of our Lord Jesus Christ, that ye have in remembrance, into how high a dignity, and to how weighty an

---

[22] *The Complete Works of John Milton, volume 3: The Shorter Poems*, edited by Barbara Kiefer Lewalski and Estelle Haan (Oxford: Oxford University Press, 2012), pp. 50-7.
[23] *The Works of the Right Reverend Father in God, Thomas Wilson, D.D., Lord Bishop of Sodor and Man* (new edition, 8 vols, Oxford: John Henry Parker, 1847-63), vol. 5, p. 217 (cited in Parsons, *The Ordinal*, p. 64).

office and charge ye are called'. It is a ministry of 'great excellency' but also of 'great difficulty', and therefore must not be entered lightly or without rigorous preparation. The dignity and weight of this work derives from the preciousness both of the Christian gospel, and of the people for whom presbyters are responsible. As the exhortation declares: 'Have always therefore printed in your remembrance, how great a treasure is committed to your charge.' The four biblical images of presbyteral ministry (messengers, watchmen, stewards, and shepherds) are paralleled in the exhortation by four biblical images of the people of God: the Lord's family, Christ's sheep, Christ's spouse, and Christ's body. Those entrusted with such treasure must fulfil their duties with the utmost care and diligence.

As the ordination service proceeds, this biblical vision for presbyteral ministry, laid down in the exhortation, is unpacked in greater detail in the examination. A series of searching questions are put to the candidates to test their suitability for the task. To these we turn in the next chapter.

2. Examination

The second essential part of the Anglican ordination service is a detailed examination, or interrogation, of the candidates.[1] Having been exhorted about the nature of the ministerial office, they are now asked serious and searching questions about their personal theological and pastoral commitment. One commentator, Dyson Hague (1857-1935), declares:

> How heart-searching are the appeals in the bishop's address!
> How subversive of all earthly ambitions and sinister designs!
> How comprehensive and penetrating the inquiries made!
> How impossible almost that any wolf in sheep's clothing
> could ever find entrance! How multiplied the precautions!
> Could prudence have erected any further safeguards? No one
> who has ever witnessed it, much less participated in it as a
> candidate for ordination, could remain insensible to its
> profitableness, its excellences, its grandeur.[2]

For deacons, presbyters, and bishops, the questions vary in number and precise wording, but may be broadly grouped together under eight headings. This public examination is designed to ensure that all those ordained to public ministry are:

1. Called by God
2. Believing the Scriptures
3. Devoted to prayer and Bible study
4. Ready to proclaim the gospel and refute error
5. Passionate for Christian unity
6. A model of godliness
7. Submitting to godly authority
8. Dependent upon the Holy Spirit

---

[1] For the influence of the Reformed theologian Martin Bucer (exiled in England 1549-51) upon the Anglican ordinal, including the form of examination questions, see Constantin Hopf, *Martin Bucer and the English Reformation* (Oxford: Blackwell, 1946), pp. 88-94; Willem van 't Spijker, *The Ecclesiastical Offices in the Thought of Martin Bucer* (Leiden: Brill, 1996), pp. 345-455.
[2] 'The Ordinal', in Dyson Hague, *The Protestantism of the Prayer Book* (third edition, London: Church Association, 1893), p. 145.

1. Called by God

Ordination candidates are first asked about their sense of vocation – not their calling by the church, but their calling by God which is then publicly recognised by the church. Responsibility for raising up and sending out workers lies not with the bishops of the Church of England but with the Lord of the harvest, and ordinands must have heard that divine call. In the *Book of Common Prayer*, deacons are asked:

> Do you trust that you are inwardly moved by the Holy Ghost to take upon you this office and ministration, to serve God for the promoting of his glory, and the edifying of his people? **Answer: I trust so.**

> Do you think that you are truly called, according to the will of our Lord Jesus Christ, and the due order of this realm, to the ministry of the Church? **Answer: I think so.**

To presbyters:

> Do you think in your heart, that you be truly called, according to the will of our Lord Jesus Christ, and the order of this Church of England, to the order and ministry of priesthood? **Answer: I think it.**

To bishops:

> Are you persuaded that you be truly called to this ministration, according to the will of our Lord Jesus Christ, and the order of this realm? **Answer: I am so persuaded.**

In *Common Worship* all candidates are asked: 'Do you believe that God is calling you to this ministry? **Answer: I do so believe.**' The question is deliberately framed in the present continuous tense ('God is calling', not 'God has called'), and stresses God's initiative by placing God as the subject.[3]

---

[3] *Ordination Services: Report of the Revision Committee*, January 2005, GS 1535Y, paragraph 53.

Here, right at the start of the interrogation, the ordinal emphasises God's action in calling the new ministers. Paul exhorted the presbyters from Ephesus to care for God's flock, 'of which the Holy Spirit has made you overseers' (Acts 20:27). Ministry begins with *vocation*, a divine call. No two people are called in exactly the same way. Every minister has a different story to tell. The prophets and apostles in Scripture, and the great pastors, preachers and missionaries in Christian history, were called to ministry in a multitude of ways – sometimes suddenly, even audibly, but often with a quiet growing sense of conviction over a number of years. Some have entered the work with overwhelming joy and eagerness, others with great hesitancy and a sense of compulsion. But there must be a call from God, and every ordinand must be able to testify to it publicly. It is too easy to drift into ordained ministry, almost by accident: increasing involvement in a local church (perhaps even a full-time apprentice scheme) leads inevitably to conversations with a vocations advisor, then meetings with a Diocesan Director of Ordinands, then a Bishops Advisory Panel, and before long you are training at theological college and deployed to a parish. The conveyor belt carries you forward from one step to the next, and you soon find yourself serving as a vicar, not quite sure how it all happened. But without a clear sense of God's call, that minister is likely to crash out when times are tough, or drift through ministry without the blessing of knowing they are where God wants them to be.

In his exposition of the ordinal before the University of Cambridge in 1811, part of his famous sermon series on *The Excellency of the Liturgy*, Charles Simeon challenged ordinands to examine their motivations very closely before entering public ministry. What was driving them? A desire for their own 'ease, honour, or preferment', or a deep concern for the souls of others? A taste for public office, or a longing above all things to advance the glory of Jesus Christ? A true sense of vocation from God, Simeon suggested, comes 'partly from a sense of obligation to him for his redeeming love, partly from a compassion for the ignorant and perishing multitudes around us, and partly from a desire to be an honoured instrument in the Redeemer's hands to establish and enlarge his kingdom in the world'.[4] Griffith Thomas acknowledged that there is no

---

[4] Charles Simeon, *The Excellency of the Liturgy; in Four Discourses, Preached before the University of Cambridge, Nov. 1811* (third edition, London: Hansard, 1816), pp. 71-2. See further, Andrew Atherstone, *Charles Simeon on the Excellency of the Liturgy* (Norwich: Joint Liturgical Studies, 2011).

precise rule for determining vocation, but offered five helpful tests: (1) do you have an intense, persistent and settled desire to enter this ministry? (2) do 'converging circumstances', practically, open the door of opportunity? (3) are you suitably qualified in terms moral character, biblical doctrine, and spiritual gifts to be a pastor and Bible teacher? (4) do your wisest Christians friends, and your local church leaders, approve? (5) have you already experienced 'a measure of blessing' from God as you have tested your gifts in evangelism, discipleship and Bible teaching? If you can answer 'Yes' to each of these five questions, it is a good indication of God's call.[5]

2. Believing the Scriptures

Ordination candidates are next interrogated about their commitment to the Holy Scriptures. In the *Book of Common Prayer*, deacons are asked two pithy questions, right at the start of their public ministries:

> Do you unfeignedly believe all the canonical Scriptures of the Old and New Testaments? **Answer: I do believe them.**

> Will you diligently read the same unto the people assembled in the church where you shall be appointed to serve? **Answer: I will.**

The first question is especially blunt. Ordinands are not asked whether they believe only some parts of the Bible, or believe it half-heartedly or hesitantly and with fingers crossed. They must publicly assent that they believe the whole of the Bible, and believe it 'unfeignedly' – that is honestly, sincerely, genuinely, as a matter of personal conviction, without pretence.

The interrogation of presbyters and bishops focuses upon one important aspect of the doctrine of Scripture, its sufficiency (compare Article 6 of the Thirty-Nine Articles):

> Are you persuaded that the Holy Scriptures contain all doctrine required of necessity for eternal salvation through faith in Jesus Christ? And are you determined, out of the said

---

[5] Thomas, *The Work of the Ministry*, pp. 112-4.

Scriptures to instruct the people committed to your charge, and to teach nothing, as required of necessity to eternal salvation, but that which you shall be persuaded may be concluded and proved by the Scripture? **Answer: I am so persuaded, and have so determined, by God's grace.**

Common Worship puts it more succinctly:

Do you accept the Holy Scriptures as revealing all things necessary to eternal salvation through faith in Jesus Christ? **Answer: I do so accept them.**

The Anglican ordinal makes clear in multiple ways that it desires to ordain Bible ministers for a Bible church. These questions echo Paul's declaration to Timothy that the Scriptures 'are able to make you wise for salvation through faith in Jesus Christ' (2 Timothy 3:15). Salvation is an eternal, not merely a temporal, concern. The Scriptures show us everything we need to know for eternal life, and for maturity in Christ, and therefore the church's ministers are to teach the Word of God, not allowing other philosophies to intrude. Archbishop Cranmer, who crafted the ordinal, wrote in the first of the Edwardian Homilies (1547) that those who want to know the way to salvation must not go running to 'the stinking puddles of men's traditions, devised by men's imagination', but come instead to 'the well of life' in the Old and New Testaments.[6] Concerning the Bible's purpose, he declared:

For the Scripture of God is the heavenly meat of our souls. The hearing and keeping of it maketh us blessed, sanctifieth us, and maketh us holy. It converteth our souls, it is a light lantern to our feet, it is a sure, a constant and a perpetual instrument of salvation, it giveth wisdom to the humble and lowly hearts, it comforteth, maketh glad, cheereth and cherisheth our conscience . . . [7]

---

[6] 'A Fruitful Exhortation to the Reading and Knowledge of Holy Scripture', in *The Book of Homilies: A Critical Edition*, edited by Gerald Bray (Cambridge: James Clarke, 2015), p. 7.
[7] 'A Fruitful Exhortation', p. 8.

The Bible is God's instrument to convert people to faith in Christ, to bring assurance of salvation, to transform our characters, to create mature churches, and to change cultures and nations. In the Church of England, the Bible is the final and authoritative Court of Appeal in all matters of doctrine and morality. Ordination candidates are expected to share that priority, allowing the Scriptures to shape the whole of their ministries. They will often have their Bibles open, not only in the pulpit but in all their pastoral care. Griffith Thomas exhorted his ordinands towards

> a first-hand experience of the Bible as the Word of God. The mind must be saturated with its truth, the heart inspired by its love, the conscience made sensitive to its law, and the will submissive to its grace. Then, then only, then always, will our life be fragrant and our ministry fruitful to the glory of God.[8]

> For the weary, the sorrowing, the despondent, the hardened, the fearing, the despairing, the Bible will naturally and necessarily be the minister's *vade mecum*, his indispensable help. And the more he studies it with this practical pastoral end in view, the more effective and the more blessed will be his ministry. Our minds and hearts should be so stored and saturated with the Bible that the Scripture view of things should instinctively be the first that occurs to us.[9]

This priority is visually demonstrated at the point of ordination itself, when ministers are each given a Bible as the necessary symbol and instrument of their pastoral and preaching office (see Chapter 3 below). Other questions in the examination also return to this theme.

3. Devoted to Prayer and Bible Study

Ordination candidates are asked not only about their public teaching. They are also questioned about the priority of prayer, and the reading and study of Scripture, as the bedrock of the minister's life. Presbyters in the *Book of Common Prayer* are asked:

---

[8] Thomas, *The Work of the Ministry*, p. 125.
[9] Thomas, *The Work of the Ministry*, pp. 127-8.

Will you be diligent in prayers, and in reading the Holy Scriptures, and in such studies as help to the knowledge of the same, laying aside the study of the world and the flesh? **Answer: I will endeavour myself so to do, the Lord being my helper.**

Likewise bishops are asked:

Will you then faithfully exercise yourself in the Holy Scriptures, and call upon God by prayer for the true understanding of the same; so that you may be able by them to teach and exhort with wholesome doctrine, and to withstand and convince the gainsayers? **Answer: I will so do, by the help of God.**

In *Common Worship* all candidates are asked:

Will you be diligent in prayer, in reading Holy Scripture, and in all studies that will deepen your faith and fit you to bear witness to the truth of the gospel? **Answer: By the help of God, I will.**

Here we see the minister not 'on duty' in the pulpit and as a leader of the liturgy, but in private devotions and personal Bible study. The apostles devoted themselves 'to prayer and to the ministry of the word' (Acts 6.4), and it is significant that prayer is listed first because without it public ministry is ineffective and quickly becomes a sham. Prayerlessness is endemic among the clergy, a symptom of fatal self-dependence. Often the pressures of public ministry squeeze out time alone with God in secret. After all, who is looking? And the end results can be catastrophic. 'It can be said without hesitation or fear of contradiction', writes Griffith Thomas, 'that ministerial weakness and, still more, ministerial unfaithfulness spring from neglect of the Bible and prayer.' The result is

awful tragedies in the ministry; the complete breakdown of character which often involves others in ruin. It will be found that these moral shipwrecks have been preceded by slow decay of spiritual life. The fall of large trees in the Broad Walk, Oxford, proclaimed rottenness long going on within

... moral spiritual decay is also traceable to neglect of private meditation of Scripture and prayer.[10]

With this in mind, ordinands must promise to be 'diligent' in prayer, and in personal study of the Scriptures. A danger for Christian professionals is always to be thinking about the next sermon, rather than what the Lord would say to them individually through his Word. Therefore Handley Moule (principal of Ridley Hall, Cambridge) urged clergy to prioritise

> such a secret study of the Word of God as shall be *unprofessional, unclerical, and simply Christian.* ... . Forget sometimes, in the name of Jesus Christ, the pulpit, the mission-room, the Bible-class; open the Bible as simply as if you were on Crusoe's island, and were destined to live and die there, alone with God.[11]

The ordination commitment to 'all studies that will deepen your faith and fit you to bear witness to the truth of the gospel' widens the lens further. It includes on-going training in order to grow more and more in ministerial effectiveness. Preparation before ordination – perhaps over two or three years via a theological college or course – is not the end but only the beginning, laying down patterns of diligent study. The minister is to be, in the jargon, a 'life-long learner'. This might mean signing up for regular conferences and diocesan training days; and spending sabbatical time reading, not just on holiday travelling the world. But it also means a commitment to proper preparation before teaching from the Scriptures. In a culture of frenetic busyness and severe pressure on the clergy diary, preparation is neglected or pushed to the margins. In the midst of pastoral crises, it can seem indulgent. But regular study time must be planned, set aside, and guarded at all costs. Of course this is partly a matter of temperament. Frederick Wynne (1827-1896), Bishop of Killaloe and Clonfert in the Church of Ireland, addressed clergy in his mid-nineteenth-century volume *The Model Parish*. To the bookish minister, who would rather be in the library than among the congregation, he urged:

---

[10] Thomas, *The Work of the Ministry*, p. 171.
[11] H. C. G. Moule, *To My Younger Brethren: Chapters on Pastoral Life and Work* (London: Hodder and Stoughton, 1892), p. 41.

> If you love your books – if it is a pleasure and a joy to you to plunge deep into them, and linger long over them, then take heed lest they become a snare to you . . . Tear yourself away sternly from your beloved volumes when the appointed hour strikes, and sally forth to that dealing with souls, for which book learning is only a preparation.

But to those disinclined to study and prepare, he advised:

> If, on the other hand, study is a weariness to you; if you would rather be stirring from place to place, walking, talking, and teaching, than sitting quietly over your Greek Testament, then you are just the person for whom diligent study is most needful. You are in danger of becoming superficial and wordy; you are in danger of dwelling exclusively on hackneyed texts, and pet doctrines, instead of 'rightly dividing the word of truth' – instead of coming to the depths and reality of things. You must discipline yourself to stick more to your study, and to labour more for your God in mind-work.[12]

As Parsons puts it: 'The fight for time to study is always on; the war must be waged – and won, by whatever means are available.'[13] Always remembering that the purpose of such study is not merely intellectual knowledge but to deepen the faith of the minister and make them more effective in handling the tool of their trade (the Bible) so that the church may be strengthened and built up.

4. Ready to Proclaim the Gospel and Refute Error

Proclamation of the gospel of Jesus Christ is a major theme running throughout the Anglican ordinal, as has already been seen. In the *Book of Common Prayer*, the ordination of presbyters concludes with this collect:

---

[12] F. R. Wynne, *The Model Parish: A Prize Essay on the Pastoral Character and Pastoral Work* (London: S. W. Partridge, 1865), p. 57 (cited in Parsons, *The Ordinal*, p. 117).
[13] Parsons, *The Ordinal*, p. 118.

Most merciful Father, we beseech thee to send upon these thy servants thy heavenly blessing; that they may be clothed with righteousness, and that thy Word spoken by their mouths may have such success, that it may never be spoken in vain. Grant also, that we may have grace to hear and receive what they shall deliver out of thy most holy Word, or agreeable to the same, as the means of our salvation; that in all our words and deeds we may seek thy glory, and the increase of thy kingdom; through Jesus Christ our Lord. Amen.

Ordained ministers are to be people with the gospel always on their lips, and mouths open to declare it. Therefore, during the interrogation of candidates, they must indicate their determination to teach the faith and act as guardians of the flock. Good pastoral care means not only many cups of tea, but also clear biblical teaching and the refuting of error. New presbyters are asked in the *Book of Common Prayer*:

Will you then give your faithful diligence always so to minister the doctrine and sacraments, and the discipline of Christ, as the Lord hath commanded, and as this Church and realm hath received the same, according to the commandments of God; so that you may teach the people committed to your cure and charge with all diligence to keep and observe the same? **Answer: I will so do, by the help of God.**

Will you be ready, with all faithful diligence, to banish and drive away all erroneous and strange doctrines contrary to God's Word; and to use both public and private monitions and exhortations, as well to the sick as to the whole, within your cures, as need shall require, and occasion shall be given? **Answer: I will, the Lord being my helper.**

New bishops are asked a similar question:

Are you ready, with all faithful diligence, to banish and drive away all erroneous and strange doctrine contrary to God's Word; and both privately and openly to call upon and encourage others to the same? **Answer: I am ready, the Lord being my helper.**

These emphases continue in *Common Worship*, though with particular focus on joyful gospel proclamation. Deacons are asked:

> Do you believe the doctrine of the Christian faith as the Church of England has received it, and in your ministry will you expound and teach it? **Answer: I believe it and will so do.**

Presbyters are asked:

> Will you lead Christ's people in proclaiming his glorious gospel, so that the good news of salvation may be heard in every place? **Answer: By the help of God, I will.**

> Will you faithfully minister the doctrine and sacraments of Christ as the Church of England has received them, so that the people committed to your charge may be defended against error and flourish in the faith? **Answer: By the help of God, I will.**

And to bishops:

> Will you lead your people in proclaiming the glorious gospel of Christ, so that the good news of salvation may be heard in every place? **Answer: By the help of God, I will.**

> Will you teach the doctrine of Christ as the Church of England has received it, will you refute error, and will you hand on entire the faith that is entrusted to you? **Answer: By the help of God, I will.**

One of the chief ways in which the 'glorious gospel of Christ' is undermined, and the 'good news of salvation' is blunted, is by the spread of erroneous or heretical teaching within the church. Sometimes it arrives as a direct assault from outside the congregation, sometimes it originates from within. This is a major concern for the New Testament authors. Paul warns the Galatians about those 'who trouble you and want to distort the gospel of Christ' (Galatians 1:7). John writes: 'For many deceivers have gone out into the world, those who do not confess the coming of Jesus Christ in the flesh' (2 John 7). The Pastoral Epistles are especially alert to the dangers of whatever is 'contrary to healthy teaching', because it leads people away from Jesus Christ causing them to make 'shipwreck' of their faith and spreads 'like gangrene' within the Christian community (1 Timothy 1:10, 19; 2 Timothy 2:17). Therefore presbyters are commanded not only to give instruction in healthy doctrine, but also to 'rebuke those who contradict it' (Titus 1:9). Proclaiming the gospel and refuting error are two sides of the same coin, and both are necessary. Sometimes that means engaging in painful controversy for the sake of the gospel. 'Contend for the faith', Jude insists (Jude 3).

The newly ordained promise that they are 'ready' both to proclaim the gospel and to refute error. To be ready means to be well-read, well-briefed, and have taken counsel with others about the most effective ways to teach and refute. To be ready means not to be caught off guard by strange doctrines, hoping they will disappear by themselves. To be ready means teaching the gospel in the parish consistently over many years, even when all seems well, so the congregation have a firm foundation – not suddenly arranging an emergency sermon series when the storm clouds have already rolled in, the crisis has arrived and it is too late. 'Faithful diligence', which presbyters and bishops promise, implies consistent effort. And their plumb-line, as always, is 'God's Word'.

'But we have to take care that we are not mere controversialists', warns Griffith Thomas, because that type of person is 'one of the most unlovely, unspiritual, and objectionable of beings. We must not wage war for the love of it, but if we find it necessary to wage it, we must do so in love.'[14] As Thomas observes, the ordinal's portrait is not of a gladiator who is full of bravado and goes looking for trouble, but of a shepherd caring for the sheep. The shepherd is happiest in times of peace, and loves nothing more than 'green pastures and quiet waters' (Psalm 23), but if the flock are in danger then the shepherd becomes fierce and wields the staff to drive away the wolf. The hired hand falls asleep on duty, or runs away (John 10:12-13), but the shepherd is willing to go into battle to save the congregation from spiritual danger.

---

[14] Thomas, *The Work of the Ministry*, p. 150.

Notice the focus in these ordination promises upon proclaiming the gospel and banishing error as essential aspects of pastoral care. This ministry is not only from the pulpit, but also in small groups and one-to-one from house to house. Presbyters are 'to use both public and private monitions and exhortations' not only with those obviously in need, but with the whole congregation. The aim is not doctrinal victory, but 'to build up the body of Christ' in maturity, 'so that we may no longer be children, tossed to and fro by the waves and carried about by every wind of doctrine, by human cunning, by craftiness in deceitful schemes.' That is why it is the responsibility of every pastor-teacher to 'speak the truth in love' (Ephesians 4.12-15).

5. Passionate for Christian Unity

The Anglican ordination service is wonderfully and biblically balanced. The promise to fight against error is swiftly followed by a promise to pursue Christian unity. As Griffith Thomas puts it: 'The minister is to be ready to wage war, and yet to maintain peace.'[15] In the *Book of Common Prayer*, new presbyters are asked:

> Will you maintain and set forwards, as much as lieth in you, quietness, peace, and love, among all Christian people, and especially among them that are or shall be committed to your charge? **Answer: I will so do, the Lord being my helper.**

A similar question is asked of new bishops (also calling them to 'correct and punish' any in their dioceses who are 'unquiet, disobedient, and criminous'). *Common Worship* rephrases the question to presbyters:

> Will you, knowing yourself to be reconciled to God in Christ, strive to be an instrument of God's peace in the Church and in the world? **Answer: By the help of God, I will.**

---

[15] Thomas, *The Work of the Ministry*, p. 156.

And to bishops:

> Will you promote peace and reconciliation in the Church and in the world; and will you strive for the visible unity of Christ's Church? **Answer: By the help of God, I will.**

Discord and disunity is destructive to the life of the church, and ordained ministers promise to take a lead in healing these divisions. They will 'strive', actively and earnestly, to promote reconciliation and peace. The Apostle Paul led by example, seeking to reconcile Euodia and Syntyche (Philippians 4:2). He urged the Ephesians – a few verses before his description of the ministry of apostles, prophets, evangelists, and pastor-teachers – to conduct themselves 'with all humility and gentleness, with patience, bearing with one another in love, eager to maintain the unity of the Spirit in the bond of peace' (Ephesians 4:2-3). Satan laughs when that spiritual unity is broken. Rivalries, factions, schisms and animosities are a plague in the church. The *Common Worship* interrogation reminds us that reconciliation is at the heart of the gospel. We are reconciled to God in Christ, through his death in our place on the cross, and are now entrusted with the urgent 'message of reconciliation' as Christ's ambassadors (2 Corinthians 5:18-21). All Christians are called to fulfil this ambassadorial role, but ordained ministers promise to make it a special priority. An unreconciled church is a contradiction of the gospel we proclaim.

The *Book of Common Prayer* emphasises reconciliation 'among all Christian people' (presbyters) and 'among all men' (bishops). *Common Worship* makes explicit that reconciliation ministry is not restricted to the church, but is also needed 'in the world'. This will include, for example, striving for peace within families and communities, as a witness to the gospel. *Common Worship* also acknowledges that harmony is needed not only within congregations, but also between congregations. Ministers too easily compete with each other, but the New Testament models collaboration and inter-dependence. Therefore in *Common Worship* every ordinand is also asked: 'Will you work with your fellow servants in the gospel for the sake of the kingdom of God?'

6. A Model of Godliness

The searching questions of the ordination examination continue. The Church of England is concerned not only for the public ministry or doctrinal correctness of its clergy, but also their personal character and the ordering of their private lives. The *Book of Common Prayer* intercessions, at the Lord's Supper, include the petition: 'Give grace, O heavenly Father, to all Bishops and Curates, that they may *both by their life and doctrine* set forth thy true and lively word.' These twin aspects belong together. Edwin Sandys (c.1519-1588), Archbishop of York, observed that some clergy 'destroy by ill teaching', but likewise other clergy, 'teaching well but living ill, do more harm by their life in one hour, than good by their doctrine in many years'.[16]

As has already been seen, the exhortation to presbyters at ordination declares:

> And seeing that ye cannot by any other means compass the doing of so weighty a work, pertaining to the salvation of man, but with doctrine and exhortation taken out of the Holy Scriptures, and with a life agreeable to the same; consider how studious ye ought to be in reading and learning the Scriptures, and in framing the manners both of yourselves, and of them that specially pertain unto you, according to the rule of the same Scriptures . . .

Here is a call to bring the whole of life, including family life, under the Word of God. It is picked up in the interrogation of ordination candidates. In the *Book of Common Prayer* ordinal, presbyters are asked:

> Will you be diligent to frame and fashion your own selves, and your families, according to the doctrine of Christ; and to make both yourselves and them, as much as in you lieth, wholesome examples and patterns to the flock of Christ?
> **Answer: I will apply myself thereto, the Lord being my helper.**

---

[16] 'The Thirteenth Sermon' (at a visitation in York), in *The Sermons of Edwin Sandys*, edited for the Parker Society by John Ayre (Cambridge: Cambridge University Press, 1842), p. 246.

A similar question is put to deacons. Meanwhile bishops are asked:

> Will you deny all ungodliness and worldly lusts, and live soberly, righteously, and godly, in this present world; that you may show yourself in all things an example of good works unto others, that the adversary may be ashamed, having nothing to say against you? **Answer: I will so do, the Lord being my helper.**

This is a direct quotation from Paul's command to Titus (borrowed from the first authorized English translation, the Great Bible of 1539; Titus 2:7-8, 11-13). The priority of personal and family godliness is likewise emphasised in the *Common Worship* ordinal. Deacons and presbyters are asked:

> Will you endeavour to fashion your own life and that of your household according to the way of Christ, that you may be a pattern and example to Christ's people? **Answer: By the help of God, I will.**

Bishops are asked:

> Will you endeavour to fashion your own life and that of your household according to the way of Christ and make your home a place of hospitality and welcome? **Answer: By the help of God, I will.**

The apostolic criteria for deacons and presbyter-bishops are laid out at length in 1 Timothy 3:1-13, a very searching passage. Only one criterion applies to ministry gifts – they must be 'able to teach' (v. 2; repeated in 2 Timothy 2:24). Paul concentrates mostly upon the personal character of those appointed to public ministry within the church. They must be faithful and consistent in their marital relationships (literally 'a one-woman man', v. 2) – careful with alcohol (vv. 3, 8), exercising self-restraint at the dinner-party, not dependent upon a glass of Rioca after a long day's work – not greedy or money-grabbing (vv. 3, 8), against which there are many warnings in Scripture like Gehazi (2 Kings 5:20-27) and Judas (John 12:6) – not violent or quarrelsome (v. 3), with unresolved anger issues. Ministers are to be impeccably honest and trustworthy, not devious or 'double-tongued' (v. 8). They are to be sober-minded (compare

Titus 2:2), not flippant; self-controlled, not ruled by their emotions and appetites; hospitable, offering refuge and welcome (a virtue especially highlighted by the *Common Worship* ordinal). In short, they are to be nothing less than 'blameless' (v. 10) and 'above reproach' (v. 2). When a minister is known for being rude, flirtatious, avaricious, bad-tempered, it is deeply damaging to their ministry and the health of the local congregation. Unrepented sin, whether public or secret, wrecks ministries. That is why the New Testament is so concerned not only for ministerial competence but ministerial character, and both deacons and presbyter-bishops must prove their ability to promote godliness in the church by their track-record in promoting godliness in the home (vv. 4, 12). What happens in the Rectory is not a private concern – it is to be a model for the Christian congregation. Therefore ordinands promise to be 'diligent' in seeking to pattern their lives, their households, and their relationships, in accordance with Christ's teaching and example.

This emphasis upon godly life, combined with biblical doctrine, is brought home clearly in some of the ordination collects, such as:

> Almighty God, giver of all good things, who by thy Holy Spirit hast appointed divers orders of ministers in thy Church; mercifully behold these thy servants now called to the office of priesthood; and replenish them so *with the truth of thy doctrine, and adorn them with innocency of life, that, both by word and good example*, they may faithfully serve thee in this office, to the glory of thy name, and the edification of thy Church; through the merits of our Saviour Jesus Christ, who liveth and reigneth with thee and the same Holy Spirit, world without end. Amen.

And this collect for new bishops:

> Most merciful Father, we beseech thee to send down upon this thy servant thy heavenly blessing; and so endue him with thy Holy Spirit, that he, preaching thy Word, may not only be earnest to reprove, beseech, and rebuke, with all patience and doctrine; *but also may be to such as believe a wholesome example*, in word, in conversation, in love, in faith, in chastity, and in purity; that, faithfully fulfilling his course, at the latter day he may receive the crown of righteousness, laid

up by the Lord the righteous judge, who liveth and reigneth one God with the Father and the Holy Ghost, world without end. Amen.

This combination of 'lip and life', or doctrine and example, is further emphasised by an explicit command that clergy take a lead in caring for the poor, the needy and the oppressed, whether inside the church or outside. In the *Common Worship* ordinal, deacons are asked:

> Will you strive to make the love of Christ known *through word and example*, and have a particular care for those in need? **Answer: By the help of God, I will.**

But this is not only a diaconal ministry. Bishops are likewise asked:

> Will you shew yourself gentle, and be merciful for Christ's sake to poor and needy people, and to all strangers destitute of help? **Answer: I will so shew myself, by God's help.** *(Book of Common Prayer)*

> Will you be gentle and merciful for Christ's sake to those who are in need, and speak for those who have no other to speak for them? **Answer: By the help of God, I will.** *(Common Worship)*

Here is a call to model godliness, in Christ's name and following Christ's example, through defence of those most in need of help, whether through unseen acts of kindness or through vocal public advocacy.

7. Submitting to Godly Authority

Paul instructs the Thessalonians: 'We ask you, brothers and sisters, to respect those who labour among you and are over you in the Lord and admonish you, and to esteem them very highly in love because of their work' (1 Thessalonians 5:12-13). Likewise the Letter to the Hebrews exhorts: 'Obey your leaders and submit to them, for they are keeping watch over your souls, as those who will have to give an account. Let them do this with joy and not with groaning, for that would be of no advantage to you' (Hebrews 13:17). Obedience to godly authority is an important aspect of Christian discipleship. It applies not only to local congregations under the oversight of ordained ministers, but also to those ordained ministers themselves. In the *Book of Common Prayer* ordinal, presbyters are asked:

> Will you reverently obey your ordinary, and other chief ministers, unto whom is committed the charge and government over you; following with a glad mind and will their godly admonitions, and submitting yourselves to their godly judgments? **Answer: I will so do, the Lord being my helper.**

The 'ordinary' is the person with legal ecclesiastical jurisdiction, usually meaning the diocesan bishop. A similar question is put to deacons, though surprisingly not to bishops (perhaps because of a sixteenth-century notion that bishops were princes of all they surveyed in their dioceses). The *Common Worship* interrogation speaks more broadly of 'the discipline of this Church'. To deacons:

> Will you accept the discipline of this Church and give due respect to those in authority? **Answer: By the help of God, I will.**

To presbyters:

> Will you accept and minister the discipline of this Church, and respect authority duly exercised within it? **Answer: By the help of God, I will.**

An equivalent question is now put, rightly, to bishops also:

> Will you accept the discipline of this Church, exercising authority with justice, courtesy and love, and always holding before you the example of Christ? **Answer: By the help of God, I will.**

These promises are not merely about the internal administration of the Church of England, but about submission to godly authority as a spiritual discipline. They take for granted that that authority will be exercised in accordance with the Word of God, as it is never right for ministers to obey directions which are contrary to Scripture. The scope of that submission is further delineated by the 'oath of canonical obedience', usually taken immediately prior to ordination, in which deacons and presbyters promise to obey their bishops not in all things, but 'in all things *lawful and honest*' (Canon C1) – that is, concerning those matters which the bishop may explicitly require by canon law (presuming, of course, that the canons are themselves consonant with Scripture).[17] *Common Worship* speaks rather prosaically of 'discipline' and 'authority'; the *Book of Common Prayer* celebrates '*godly* admonitions' (which may include rebuke and warning, as well as exhortation) and '*godly* judgments'. The promised submission is not to be with grumbling, or extracted grudgingly, nor even with cold legalism, but with '*a glad mind and will*'. Here is a beautiful picture of a healthy church in which ordained ministers cheerfully welcome the godly oversight of those placed over them in the Lord, for the flourishing of ministries and congregations.

An ordination collect for new bishops, for the exercise of godly authority

Almighty God, and most merciful Father, who of thine infinite goodness hast given thine only and dearly beloved Son Jesus Christ, to be our redeemer, and the author of everlasting life; who, after that he had made perfect our redemption by his death, and was ascended into heaven, poured down his gifts abundantly upon men, making some apostles, some prophets, some evangelists, some pastors and doctors, to the edifying and making perfect his Church; *grant, we beseech thee, to this thy servant such grace, that he may evermore be ready to spread abroad thy gospel, the glad tidings of reconciliation with thee; and use the authority given him, not to destruction, but to salvation; not to hurt, but to help:* so that as a wise and faithful servant, giving to thy family their portion in due season, he may at last be received into everlasting joy; through the same Jesus Christ our Lord, who, with thee and the Holy Ghost, liveth and reigneth, one God, world without end. Amen.

---

[17] Rupert Bursell, 'The Oath of Canonical Obedience', *Ecclesiastical Law Journal* vol. 16 (May 2014), pp. 168-86; Gerald Bray, *The Oath of Canonical Obedience* (London: Latimer Trust, 2004).

8. Dependent on the Holy Spirit

When the Apostle Paul describes his ministry, commissioned by God to preach the gospel of Christ, he exclaims: 'Who is sufficient for these things?' (2 Corinthians 2:16). As has been seen throughout the ordination exhortation and examination, the ministry is weighty and the standard for ministers is set remarkably high. Thus it is right to be driven to our knees, seeking the Lord's mercy and grace. Dependence upon God is a keynote of the whole ordination service. Each promise during the examination – to teach the truth, banish error, seek unity, pray diligently, model godliness, obey authority – is framed with words such as 'I will so do, *the Lord being my helper*' *(Book of Common Prayer)* and '*By the help of God*, I will' *(Common Worship)*.

In the exhortation to presbyters in the *Book of Common Prayer*, they are urged to 'pray earnestly' for God's Holy Spirit. And again: 'continually pray to God the Father, by the mediation of our only Saviour Jesus Christ, for the heavenly assistance of the Holy Ghost'. Otherwise this weighty work is impossible. As soon as they have made their examination promises, the bishop prays that the Lord by his grace would grant them the necessary strength (including words from Philippians 1:6):

> Almighty God, who hath given you this will to do all these things; grant also unto you strength and power to perform the same, that he may accomplish his work which he hath begun in you; through Jesus Christ our Lord. Amen.

This dependence upon the Holy Spirit is made doubly explicit in *Common Worship* by the final question in the examination itself, echoing Paul's reminder to Timothy to fan into flame, or 'stir up', the gift of God within him (1 Timothy 1:6). To deacons:

> Will you then, in the strength of the Holy Spirit, continually stir up the gift of God that is in you, to grow in holiness and grace? **Answer: By the help of God, I will.**

To presbyters:

> Will you then, in the strength of the Holy Spirit, continually stir up the gift of God that is in you, to make Christ known

among all whom you serve? **Answer: By the help of God, I will.**

Deacons and presbyters are then exhorted:

> You cannot bear the weight of this calling in your own strength, but only by the grace and power of God. Pray therefore that your heart may daily be enlarged and your understanding of the Scriptures enlightened. Pray earnestly for the gift of the Holy Spirit.

Stephen was 'full of grace and power' (Acts 6:8) and is thus also, like Timothy, a model for Anglican ministers. A similar question is put to bishops, followed by a similar exhortation (picking up Romans 8:29 and Romans 12:1):

> Will you then, in the strength of the Holy Spirit, continually stir up the gift of God that is in you, that the good news of Christ may be proclaimed in all the world? **Answer: By the help of God, I will.**

> . . . You cannot bear the weight of this calling in your own strength, but only by the grace and power of God. Pray therefore that you may be conformed more and more to the image of God's Son, so that through the outpouring of the Holy Spirit your life and ministry may be made holy and acceptable to God. Pray earnestly for the gift of the Holy Spirit.

Without the empowering of the Holy Spirit, every ministry in the church would be a fruitless failure. Therefore ordinands must declare their utter dependence on the Lord. At the ordination of presbyters and bishops, the examination is followed fittingly by a direct invocation of the Spirit in the ancient hymn *Veni Creator Spiritus*.

3. ORDINATION

After the candidates have been exhorted and thoroughly examined, we reach the third and final part of the liturgy, the moment of ordination itself. *Veni Creator Spiritus* ('Come, Holy Ghost, our souls inspire') leads naturally to invocation of the Spirit upon the candidates, with the laying-on-of-hands.[1]

The formula in the *Book of Common Prayer* is a mix between a prayer to God and a charge to the ordinands:

> Receive the Holy Ghost for the office and work of a priest in the Church of God, now committed unto thee by the imposition of our hands. Whose sins thou dost forgive, they are forgiven; and whose sins thou dost retain, they are retained. And be thou a faithful dispenser of the Word of God, and of his holy sacraments; in the name of the Father, and of the Son, and of the Holy Ghost. Amen.

The formula *Accipite Spiritum Sanctum* began to appear in ordinals from the thirteenth century, translated by Cranmer as 'Receive the Holy Ghost' (John 20:22). But he linked it unambiguously with Jesus' commission of the apostles into public ministry, by also adding the rest of the quotation about 'forgiving' and 'retaining' sins (John 20:23). In its biblical context, this is not a reference to the ministry of confession and absolution, but is a shorthand way of describing the ministry of gospel proclamation which calls upon people to repent and believe in Jesus Christ, parallel to the Great Commissions in Luke 24:45-49 and Matthew 28:18-20.[2] The formula used at the consecration of a bishop echoes instead Paul's commission to Timothy in 2 Timothy 1:6-7:

---

[1] Surprisingly, in the *Book of Common Prayer* the Holy Spirit is not invoked upon deacons, an anomaly corrected in *Common Worship*.

[2] See further, T. W. Drury, *Confession and Absolution: The Teaching of the Church of England as Interpreted and Illustrated by the Writings of the Reformers of the Sixteenth Century* (London: Hodder and Stoughton, 1903), pp. 9-14, 27-39, 247-50; Andrew Atherstone, *'I Absolve You': Private Confession and the Church of England* (London: Latimer Trust, 2005).

Receive the Holy Ghost for the office and work of a bishop in the Church of God, now committed unto thee by the imposition of our hands; in the name of the Father, and of the Son, and of the Holy Ghost. Amen. And remember that thou stir up the grace of God, which is given thee by this imposition of our hands; for God hath not given us the spirit of fear, but of power, and love, and soberness.

There is no suggestion that presbyters and bishops have previously lacked the Holy Spirit, since of course every Christian receives the gift of the Spirit at their conversion (Romans 8:9; 1 Corinthians 12:13). Instead, it concerns the equipping of the Spirit for their new ministries. This is made clear by an important linguistic change. Where Cranmer's 1552 ordinal simply had, 'Receive the Holy Ghost' or 'Take the Holy Ghost', which was open to misunderstanding, the 1662 ordinal inserted the words '*for the office and work of a [priest / bishop] in the Church of God'.* It is a prayer for spiritual anointing for a particular ministry.

Nor should we understand the imposition of hands to be automatically effectual – the anointing is determined, of course, by the Holy Spirit not by the ordaining bishop! In answer to puritan objections, John Whitgift (c.1530-1604), later Archbishop of Canterbury, explained:

To use these words, 'Receive the Holy Ghost', in ordering of ministers, which Christ himself used in appointing his apostles, is no more ridiculous and blasphemous than it is to use the words that he used in the supper. . . . The bishop by speaking these words doth not take upon him to give the Holy Ghost, no more than he doth to remit sins, when he pronounceth the remission of sins; but by speaking these words of Christ . . . he doth shew the principal duty of a minister, and assureth him of the assistance of God's Holy Spirit, if he labour in the same accordingly.[3]

---

[3] 'Defence of the Answer to the Admonition' (1574), Tract 4, 'Of ministers having no pastoral charge; of ceremonies used in ordaining ministers; of apostles, evangelists, and prophets', in *The Works of John Whitgift*, edited for the Parker Society by John Ayre (3 vols, Cambridge: Cambridge University hPress, 1851-53), vol. 1, p. 489.

Nevertheless, for the sake of clarity, *Common Worship* helpfully reformulates the invocation of the Spirit as a brief prayer: 'Send down the Holy Spirit on your servant *N*, for the office and work of a [deacon / priest / bishop] in your Church.' It is also worth noticing that although the ordination is conducted locally under the auspices of the Church of England, it is not a sectarian or denominational action, but is ordination to public ministry in 'the Church of God'.

Priests or Presbyters?

Unlike many other Reformation churches, the Church of England chose to retain the three traditional orders of ministry and the three traditional names for them – deacons, priests, and bishops.[4] These names are derived etymologically from the New Testament – deacon from *diakonos*; priest from *presbyteros* via the Old English *prest*; and bishop from *episkopos* via the Old English *biscop*.[5] Perhaps because of this direct New Testament association, Thomas Cranmer's 1552 ordinal speaks of 'priests' and 'priesthood', carried over into the 1662 *Book of Common Prayer*.

However, during the middle ages the word 'priest' also came to have sacerdotal associations, synonymous with the Latin *sacerdos*, the person responsible for offering sacrifices to God, especially at the mass. Therefore in all major English Bible translations from William Tyndale in 1526 onwards, 'priest' has been used to denote those responsible for Old Testament temple sacrifice (Hebrew *kohen*, Greek *hiereus*), while the New Testament *presbyteros* is translated 'presbyter' or 'elder'. The New Testament uses *hiereus* of Jesus Christ our 'great high priest' (Hebrews 2:17, 4:14) and of the whole people of God, a 'royal priesthood' (1 Peter

---

[4] For the evolution of three orders in the early church, see Roger Beckwith, *Elders in Every City: The Origin and Role of the Ordained Ministry* (Carlisle: Paternoster, 2003). For a suggestion that the Anglican ordinal teaches only *one* order of ministry, divided into three sub-orders (with deacons as apprentice presbyters), see Tim Patrick, 'The Pastoral Offices in the Pastoral Epistles and the Church of England's First Ordinal', in *Paul as Pastor*, edited by Brian Rosner, Andrew Malone and Trevor Burke (London: Bloomsbury, 2018), pp. 159-82.
[5] See, for example, etymologies in the *Oxford English Dictionary*. For suggestion of an alternative etymology of 'priest', via Old English, from Latin *praepositus* (the person in charge), see *Chambers Dictionary of Etymology*, edited by Robert K. Barnhart (Edinburgh: Chambers, 1988), p. 838.

2:5, 9; Revelation 1:5, 5:10).[6] But the word is never used in the New Testament to describe Christian ministry, which is fundamentally pastoral and proclamatory, not sacerdotal or mediatorial. The Roman Catholic Douai-Rheims New Testament of 1582, translating from the Latin Vulgate into English, used 'priest' interchangeable for both these offices, which brought forth the protest of William Fulke (c.1536-1589), master of Pembroke College, Cambridge, in his *Defence of the Sincere and True Translations* (1583):

> you corruptly translate *sacerdos* and *presbyter* always, as though they were all one, a *priest*, as though the Holy Ghost had made that distinction in vain, or that there were no difference between the priesthood of the New Testament and the Old. The name of priest, according to the original derivation from *presbyter*, we do not refuse: but according to the common acception for a sacrificer, we cannot take it, when it is spoken of the ministry of the New Testament. And although many of the ancient fathers have abusively confounded the terms *sacerdos* and *presbyter*, yet that is no warrant for us to translate the scripture, and to confound that which we see manifestly the Spirit of God has distinguished.[7]

Here is the conundrum. The Anglican ordinal interprets the order of 'priests' in line with New Testament presbyteral ministry – as seen clearly in the exhortation and examination. They are messengers, sentinels, stewards, shepherds, with primary responsibility to pastor the flock and teach the Scriptures. They have no sacrificial functions. Indeed the *Book of Common Prayer* is careful in its Holy Communion liturgy to avoid terms like 'altar', 'sacrifice', and 'offering' as contradicting the gospel of grace.[8] The 'priests' of the Church of England are therefore quite unlike

---

[6] For historical context, see Malcolm B. Yarnell III, *Royal Priesthood in the English Reformation* (Oxford: Oxford University Press, 2013).

[7] William Fulke, *A Defence of the Sincere and True Translations of the Holy Scriptures into the English Tongue, Against the Cavils of Gregory Martin*, edited for the Parker Society by Charles Henry Hartshorne (Cambridge: Cambridge University Press, 1843), p. 109.

[8] See further, Andrew Atherstone, 'The Lord's Supper and the Gospel of Salvation: Grace Alone and Faith Alone in the *Book of Common Prayer*', in *Feed My Sheep: The Anglican Ministry of Word and Sacrament*, edited by Lee Gatiss (London: Lost Coin, 2016), pp. 71-99.

either the 'priests' of the Old Testament or the 'priests' of the Church of Rome. And yet the same name is used of two distinct functions, leading to endless confusion. Where Greek and Latin have two words, English commonly uses only one. This is seen, for example, when comparing the English and Latin versions of the Thirty-Nine Articles. Article 31 denounces the 'priest' (in Latin *sacerdos*) who offers the sacrifice of the mass, but Article 32 affirms that 'priests' (in Latin *presbyteri*) may marry.[9]

The dilemma has been debated since the sixteenth century. The obvious objection to retaining the word 'priest' in the Anglican formularies was laid out in the 1570s by the puritan Thomas Cartwright (c.1534-1603), former Lady Margaret Professor of Divinity at Cambridge, during the Admonition Controversy. He noted that in common English parlance, and in all English Bible translations, the word 'priest' signified 'not a minister of the gospel, but a sacrificer, which the minister of the gospel is not; therefore we ought not to call the ministers of the gospel "priests".'[10] But John Whitgift replied that at the reformation of the Church of England any sacrificial meaning had been dropped, so there was no longer need to avoid the word 'priest':

> the very word itself, as it is used in our English tongue, soundeth the word *presbyter.* As heretofore use hath made it to be taken for a sacrifice, so will use now alter that signification, and make it to be taken for a minister of the gospel. But it is mere vanity to contend for the name when we agree of the thing: the name may be used, and not used, without any great offence.[11]

---

[9] *Documents of the English Reformation, 1526-1701*, edited by Gerald Bray (Cambridge: James Clark, 2004), p. 303.

[10] Quoted in 'Defence of the Answer to the Admonition' (1574), Tract 21: 'Of subscribing to the communion-book', in *The Works of John Whitgift*, vol. 3, p. 351.

[11] 'Defence of the Answer to the Admonition' (1574), Tract 21, in *The Works of John Whitgift*, vol. 3, p. 351. See further, Andrew Cinnamond, 'Diversity in the Reformed English Tradition: An Introduction to the Admonition Controversy, 1572-77' (PhD thesis, Middlesex University, 2012), and Andrew Cinnamond, *What Matters in Reforming the Church? Puritan Grievances Under Elizabeth I* (London: Latimer Trust, 2011).

Richard Hooker (1554-1600) in his *Lawes of Ecclesiastical Polity* agreed that the Church of England could retain the word 'priest' with a clear conscience, because ordained ministry had been shorn of its sacrificial connotations. Congregations no longer thought of their 'priests' in that way, he argued, just as they no longer assumed a 'senator' or 'alderman' was an old man. The meanings of words change. He did not want to make it a big issue and was content for 'priest' and 'presbyter' to be used interchangeably (as they now are in the *Common Worship* ordinal). Nevertheless, Hooker's personal preference, for the sake of theological clarity, was 'presbyter': 'in truth the word *Presbyter* doth seem more fit, and in propriety of speech more agreeable than *Priest* with the drift of the whole Gospel of Jesus Christ. . . . The Holy Ghost throughout the body of the New Testament making so much mention of them doth not any where call them Priests.'[12]

Whitgift and Hooker were overly optimistic that in the post-Reformation church, the word 'priest' could be reclaimed unequivocally for its original meaning as 'presbyter'. However, the subsequent history of Anglicanism has proved them wrong – 'priest' still remains a highly ambiguous and contested word under which all manner of incompatible theologies have been smuggled into the Church of England. Our English Bible translations compound the issue by connecting 'priesthood' with Old Testament sacrifice, leaving congregations confused or misled when their clergy are called 'priests'. Therefore, rather than seeking to define 'priest' every time we use the word, a more fruitful approach is to speak explicitly of 'presbyters' when New Testament Christian ministry is meant.

The Gift of the Bible

If the key visual symbol of ordination is the laying-on-of-hands (associated with anointing by the Holy Spirit), by ancient custom is it immediately followed by 'the porrection' – *porrectio instrumentorum* – the ritual presentation of objects associated with the ordinand's new ministry.

In medieval ordinals, deacons were given the Gospel Book, because reading the Gospel in public worship was one of their duties. At the Reformation, Cranmer expanded this symbolic gift from the Gospel Book to the whole New Testament, with the words: 'Take thou authority to read

---

[12] Richard Hooker, *Lawes of Ecclesiastical Polity*, book 5, chapter 78.2-3.

the Gospel in the Church of God, and to preach the same, if thou be thereto licensed by the bishop himself'. For many centuries, in Anglican tradition, deacons were given a Greek New Testament, as a reminder to study God's Word in the original language not merely in translation.

Priests in the middle ages were given a chalice (communion cup) and paten (communion plate), symbolizing the sacramental dimension of their ministry. In 1550 Cranmer added the Bible (Old and New Testaments) into the mix, so priests received the Bible in one hand and the chalice and paten in the other, with the instruction: 'Take thou authority to preach the Word of God, and to minister the holy sacraments in the congregation, where thou shalt be so appointed'.[13] But in a particularly significant revision, from 1552 (followed by the 1662 ordinal) the ordination gift to priests was the Bible alone. Although the gospel word and gospel sacrament belong together, Cranmer made this important change to ensure the Bible's pre-eminence at Anglican ordinations. Thus the *Book of Common Prayer* ordinal hammers home the point that the Church of England is a Bible church, and presbyteral ministry is a ministry of the word.

The Reformation brought similar revisions to the consecration of bishops. In 1550 Cranmer dropped the anointing with oil, and the presentation of episcopal ring and mitre – leaving only two parts of the *porrectio instrumentorum*, the Bible and the pastoral staff. But in 1552 the pastoral staff was also omitted, leaving the Bible only as the symbol of the bishop's office. The new bishop, on being handed the book, is exhorted with words borrowed from 1 Timothy 4:13-16:

> Give heed unto reading, exhortation, and doctrine. Think upon the things contained in this book. Be diligent in them, that the increase coming thereby may be manifest unto all men. Take heed unto thyself, and to doctrine, and be diligent

---

[13] In 1662, following the administrative chaos of the Commonwealth period, this was revised to 'where thou shalt be *lawfully* appointed thereunto', as a reminder that presbyters could not minister wherever they chose but only where lawfully sent, which in normal circumstance meant under bishop's licence. For the principle of being 'lawfully called and sent', see Article 23 of the Thirty-Nine Articles.

in doing them: for by so doing thou shalt both save thyself
and them that hear thee . . .

In *Common Worship* the gift of the Bible maintains its pre-eminent
place, immediately after the ordination prayer:

> Receive this book, as a sign of the authority given you this day
> to speak God's word to his people. Build them up in his truth
> and serve them in his name. *(CW deacons)*

> Receive this book, as a sign of the authority which God has
> given you this day to preach the gospel of Christ and to
> minister his holy sacraments. *(CW presbyters)*

> Receive this book, as a sign of the authority given you this day
> to build up Christ's Church in truth. Here are words of
> eternal life. Take them for your guide and declare them to the
> world. *(CW bishops)*

Recent tendencies to insert additional symbolic gifts into the ordination
service should be resisted. As Cranmer realized, the supremacy of
Scripture is diluted when it becomes merely one of several instruments,
rather than the single gift. Likewise the intrusion of ritual acts which
suggest ordination to a sacerdotal ministry (such as anointing of the
ordinand's hands, prostration before the 'altar', concelebration, or the
donning of sacerdotal garments) should be resisted.[14] These symbolic
gifts and actions have become popular in some dioceses in recent years,
but they suggest a return to pre-Reformation ordination liturgies and
mask the gospel clarity of the traditional Anglican ordination service. The
Anglican ordinal, from beginning to end, is a wonderful gospel liturgy
drenched in biblical imagery – its reiterated focus is pastoral and
preaching ministry, with the Word of God and the good news of Jesus
Christ at its heart. The gift of the Bible, and the Bible alone, to the newly
ordained is the symbolic capstone of all that precedes it.

---

[14] See further, Andrew Atherstone, *Scarf or Stole at Ordination? A Plea for the
Evangelical Conscience* (London: Latimer Trust, 2012).

Conclusion

The Anglican ordinal is the best handbook for Anglican ministry, a beautiful description of theological priorities and ministry models for today's Church. Its three key constituents – Exhortation, Examination, Ordination – draw deeply upon biblical themes. Anglican clergy are called to public ministry as messengers, sentinels, stewards, and shepherds. This is a weighty and awesome responsibility, caring for the people of God, declaring the good news, seeking the lost, protecting the flock from danger, and feeding them the Word of God. Therefore searching questions and solemn promises seek to test the suitability of those who offer themselves for this ministry. Are they called by God? Do they believe the Scriptures? Are they devoted to prayer and Bible study? Are they ready to proclaim the gospel and refute error? Are they passionate for Christian unity? Do they model godliness? Do they submit to godly authority? Are they dependent upon the Holy Spirit? Those who are proven in these areas are welcomed into ordained Anglican ministry with great delight and communal celebration – invocation of the Holy Spirit with the laying-on-of-hands, seeking God's anointing on their new ministries, and the gift of the Bible as the visual symbol of their pastoral and preaching office. This ministry is a precious gift of God to the Church, designed for the Church's health, growth and well-being. We need an abundant supply of Anglican clergy of the personal character and ministerial competence demanded by the Anglican ordinal, and we look to the Lord to raise them up. 'The harvest is plentiful, but the labourers are few. Therefore pray earnestly to the Lord of the harvest to send out labourers into his harvest fields' (Matthew 9:37-38).

Anglican Foundations Series

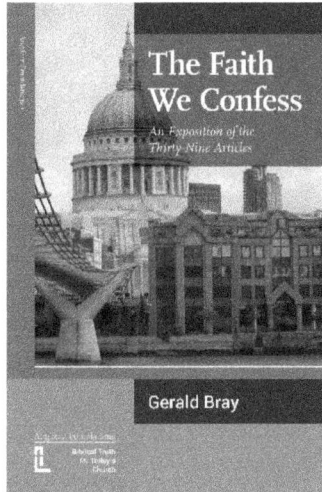

The Anglican Foundations series are a collection of booklets which offer practical guidance on Church of England liturgy and doctrine.

These include:
- *The Faith We Confess: An exposition of the Thirty-Nine Articles*
- *The 'Very Pure Word of God: The Book of Common Prayer as a model of biblical liturgy*
- *Dearly Beloved: Building God's people through morning and evening prayer*
- *Day by Day: The rhythm of the Bible in the Book of Common Prayer*
- *The Supper: Cranmer and Communion*
- *A Fruitful Exhortation: A guide to the Homilies*
- *Instruction in the Way of the Lord: A guide to the catechism*
- *Till Death Do Us Part: "The solemnization of Matrimony" in the Book of Common Prayer*
- *Sure and Certain Hope: Death and burial*
- *The Athanasian Creed*
- *The Anglican Ordinal: Gospel Priorities for Church of England Ministry*

Recently Released by the Latimer Trust

The Athanasian Creed by *Martin Davie*

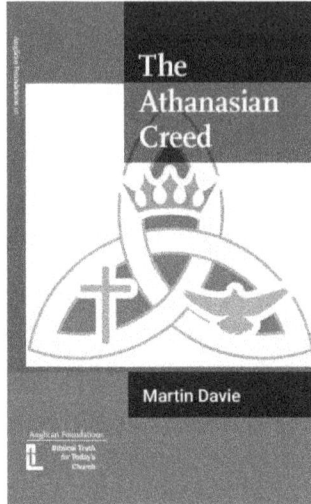

The Athanasian Creed is now the neglected Creed. Most of the laity do not know about it, its theology is not well understood even by the clergy, and it is almost never used in services, even in conservative churches.

This book's aim is to counter this neglect of the Athanasian Creed. Its five chapters:

- Set out what kind of document the Creed is and when and why it was written;
- Give a detailed commentary on the Creed, explaining clearly what it teaches and why what it teaches is true;
- Explain why the Creed still matters today, not only because of its importance in the history of Christian theology and liturgy, but primarily because of the continuing significance of its teaching.
- Explore how people in the Church of England today can be encouraged to make use of the Creed both in theological education and in the everyday life of their parishes.

Synods by *Gerald Bray*

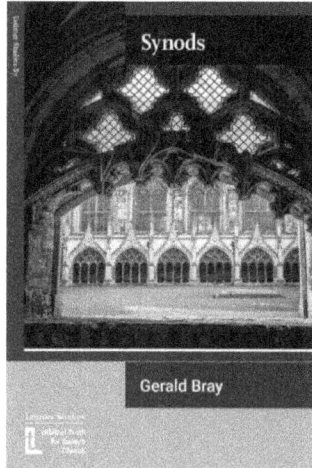

Synods are gatherings of church officers that convene for the purpose of deliberating what church policy should be. Their agenda may include resolving disputes that have arisen as well, as making plans for the future development of the life of the church.

They are typically representative bodies, though who they represent varies from time to time and from church to church. They have been held from the very earliest days of Christianity, and for many centuries they were understood to be assemblies of bishops. That is still the case in the Roman Catholic and Eastern Orthodox churches, but Anglican practice is much broader in scope, including clergy and laity as well. Modern synods also meet on a regular basis and operate according to a fixed constitution. They share some features in common with those of other times and places, but they are not direct descendants of any particular ancient tradition. There is no form of Anglican synodical government beyond the level of the national church, a fact that has become increasingly problematic in the worldwide Anglican Communion. Reform of the national synodical structure and the development of an effective form of synodical government that will be regarded as authoritative by the entire Communion are the greatest challenges we face today and it is these that this essay seeks to address.

www.ingramcontent.com/pod-product-compliance
Lightning Source LLC
Chambersburg PA
CBHW032059040426
42449CB00007B/1139